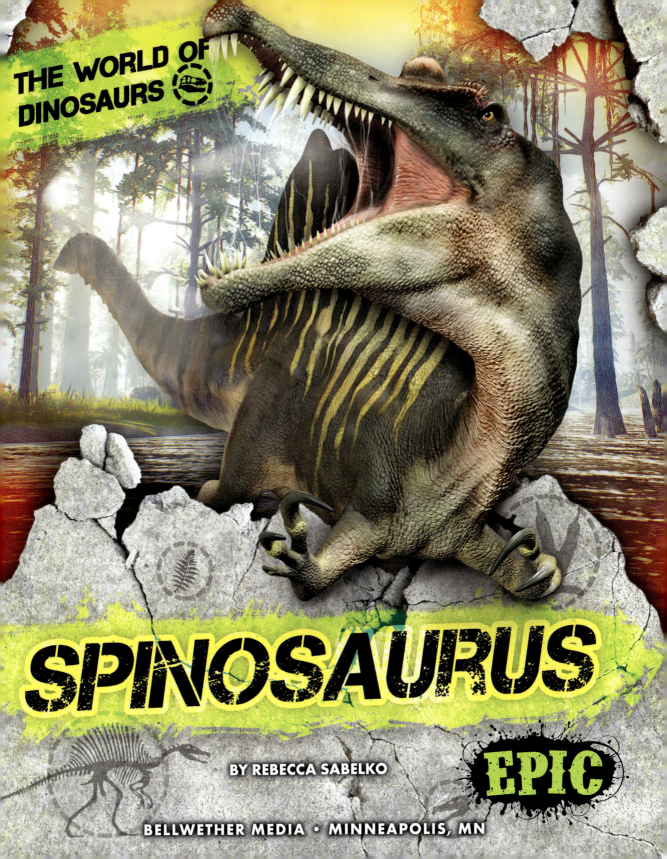

SPINOSAURUS

BY REBECCA SABELKO

EPIC

BELLWETHER MEDIA • MINNEAPOLIS, MN

EPIC

EPIC BOOKS are no ordinary books. They burst with intense action, high-speed heroics, and shadows of the unknown. Are you ready for an Epic adventure?

This edition first published in 2021 by Bellwether Media, Inc.

No part of this publication may be reproduced in whole or in part without written permission of the publisher. For information regarding permission, write to Bellwether Media, Inc., Attention: Permissions Department, 6012 Blue Circle Drive, Minnetonka, MN 55343.

Library of Congress Cataloging-in-Publication Data

LC record for Spinosaurus available at https://lccn.loc.gov/2020048049

Text copyright © 2021 by Bellwether Media, Inc. EPIC and associated logos are trademarks and/or registered trademarks of Bellwether Media, Inc.

Editor: Betsy Rathburn   Designer: Jeffrey Kollock

Printed in the United States of America, North Mankato, MN.

TABLE OF CONTENTS

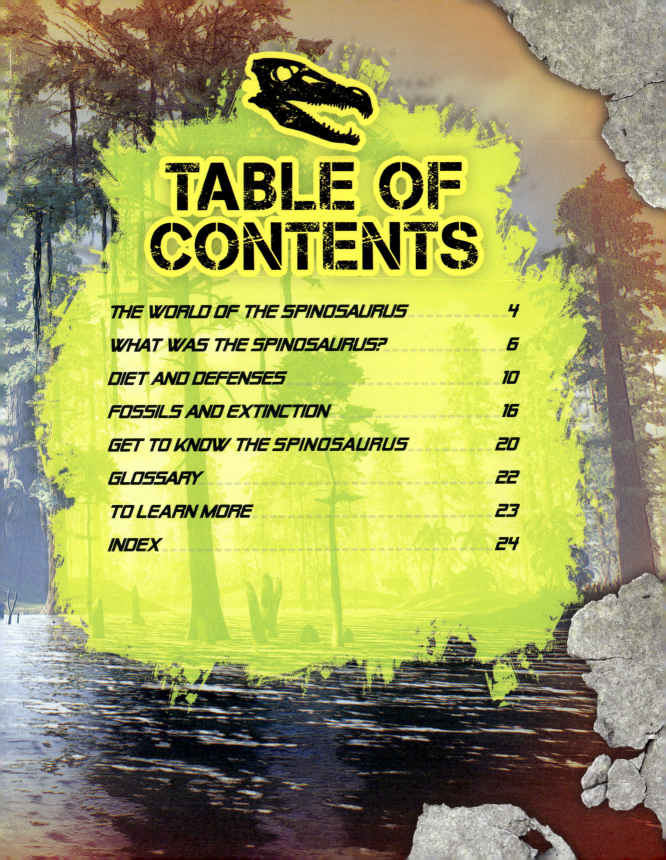

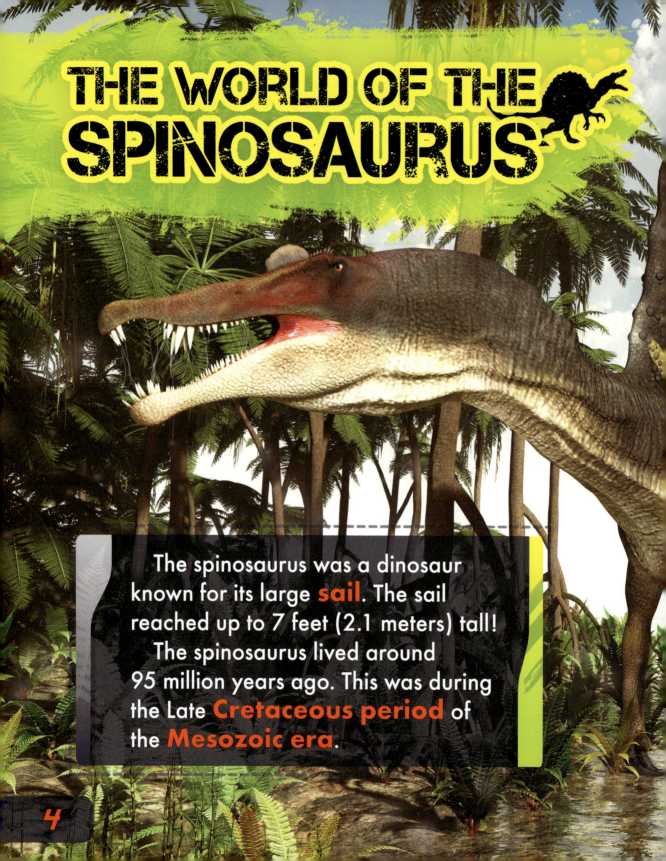

THE WORLD OF THE SPINOSAURUS

The spinosaurus was a dinosaur known for its large **sail**. The sail reached up to 7 feet (2.1 meters) tall! The spinosaurus lived around 95 million years ago. This was during the Late **Cretaceous period** of the **Mesozoic era**.

sail

Late Cretaceous period

PRONUNCIATION

SPINE-o-SAWR-us

WHAT WAS THE SPINOSAURUS?

The spinosaurus was one of the largest **theropods** on Earth! It grew up to 50 feet (15.2 meters) long.

It was the only known dinosaur to live both on land and in water.

SIZE CHART

| | 25 feet (7.6 meters) |
| 15 feet (4.6 meters) |
| 5 feet (1.5 meters) |

The spinosaurus spent a lot of time in water. It used its **webbed** feet like paddles.

webbed feet

⚠️ *NAME GAME*

The word *spinosaurus* means "spined lizard."

It waved its wide tail in an S motion.
This helped it speed through water!

DIET AND DEFENSES

snout

⚠ LONG CLAWS

The spinosaurus had long claws. It used its claws to hook prey!

The spinosaurus mostly ate fish. Its long nose was like a crocodile's **snout**. Long teeth filled its mouth.

Its teeth and jaws helped the dinosaur hold on to its slippery **prey**!

SPINOSAURUS DIET

fish

sharks

11

The spinosaurus likely had special **sensors** in its long snout. Crocodiles have similar sensors today.

The sensors helped the dinosaur know when to strike. They sensed the movements of fish.

13

This dinosaur was a top **predator**. It was not hunted by other dinosaurs. Its tall sail may have acted as a warning. The sail kept other hunters away.

FOSSILS AND EXTINCTION

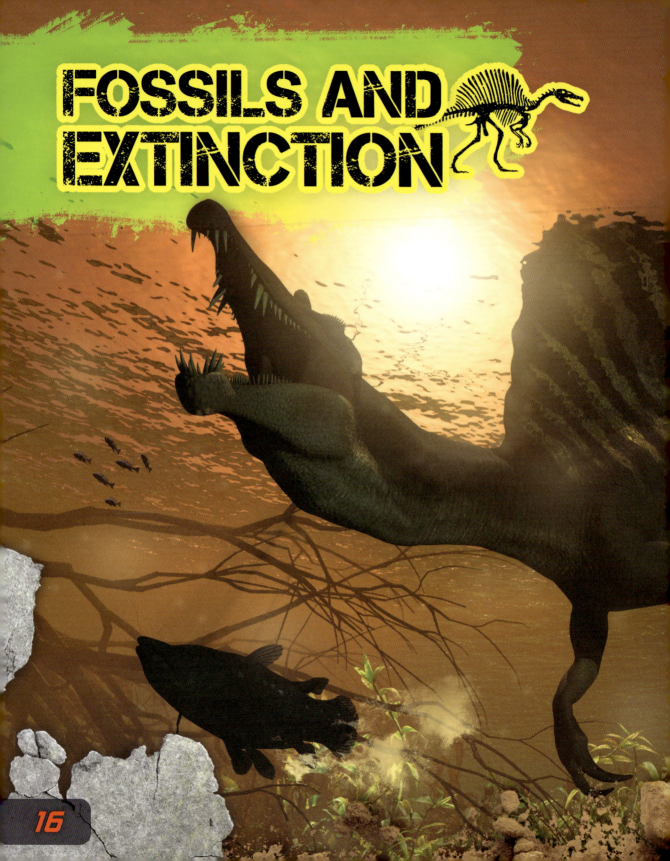

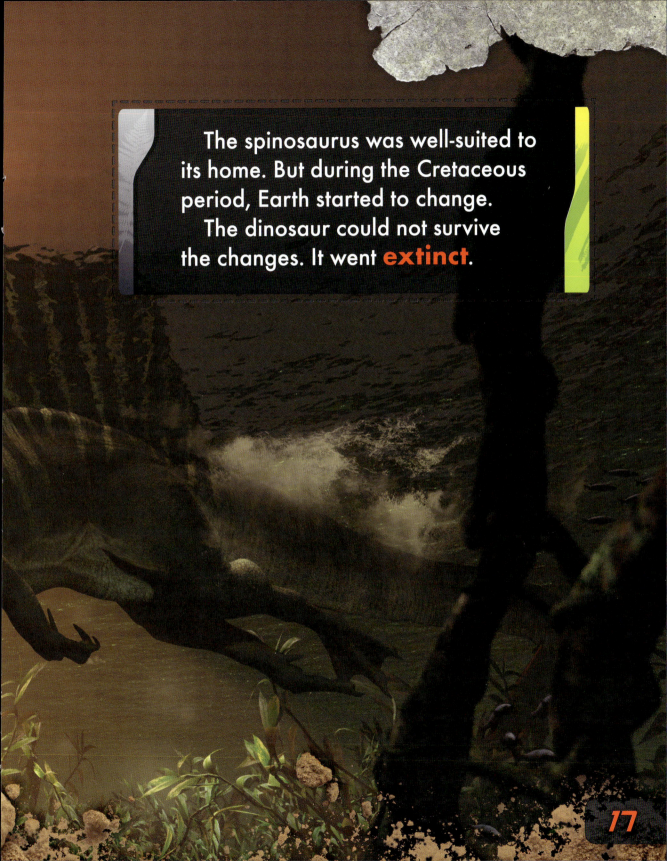

The spinosaurus was well-suited to its home. But during the Cretaceous period, Earth started to change. The dinosaur could not survive the changes. It went **extinct**.

The first spinosaurus **fossils** were found in Egypt in 1912. Others have been found across northern Africa.

⚠️ **LOST FOSSILS**

The first spinosaurus fossils ever found were destroyed in a World War II bombing.

SPINOSAURUS FOSSIL MAP

Africa

South America

KEY

⊙— fossil site

Scientists continue to study spinosaurus fossils. They learn more about how this dinosaur lived!

GET TO KNOW THE SPINOSAURUS

sail

NAMED BY

Ernst Stromer

long snout

FOOD

sharks

fish

HEIGHT up to 20 feet (6.1 meters) tall

LENGTH up to 50 feet (15.2 meters) long

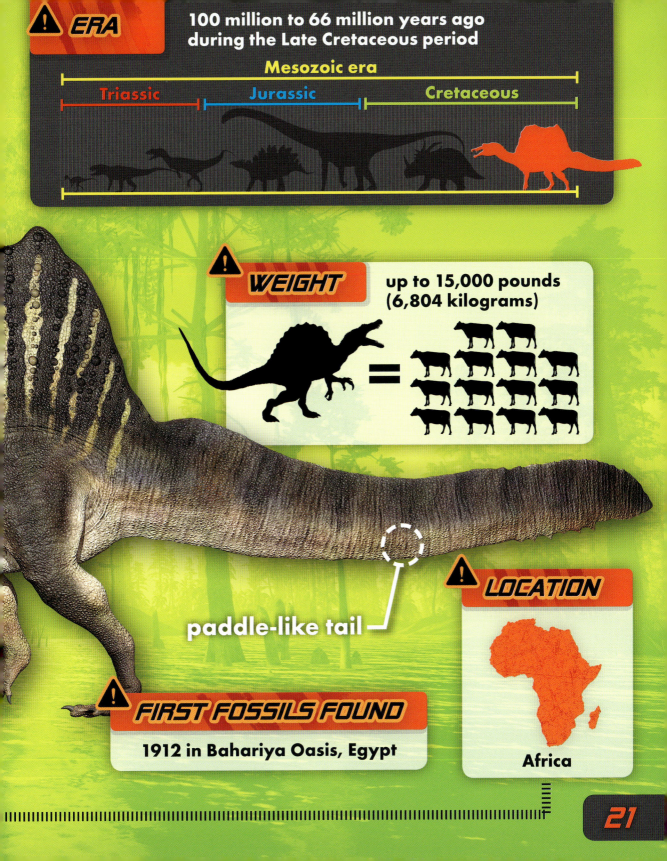

⚠ ERA

100 million to 66 million years ago during the Late Cretaceous period

Mesozoic era

Triassic | Jurassic | Cretaceous

⚠ WEIGHT

up to 15,000 pounds (6,804 kilograms)

=

paddle-like tail

⚠ LOCATION

Africa

⚠ FIRST FOSSILS FOUND

1912 in Bahariya Oasis, Egypt

GLOSSARY

Cretaceous period—the last period of the Mesozoic era that occurred between 145 million and 66 million years ago; the Late Cretaceous period began around 100 million years ago.

extinct—no longer living

fossils—the remains of living things that lived long ago

Mesozoic era—a time in history in which dinosaurs lived on Earth; the first birds, mammals, and flowering plants appeared on Earth during the Mesozoic era.

predator—an animal that hunts other animals for food

prey—animals eaten by other animals for food

sail—the long spikes connected by skin that grew out of the back of the spinosaurus

sensors—body parts that sense movement

snout—the nose of some animals

theropods—meat-eating dinosaurs that had two small arms and moved on two legs

webbed—related to thin skin between the toes of some animals

TO LEARN MORE

AT THE LIBRARY

Bell, Samantha S. *Spinosaurus*. Lake Elmo, Minn.: Focus Readers, 2018.

Braun, Eric. *Could You Survive the Cretaceous Period?: An Interactive Prehistoric Adventure*. North Mankato, Minn.: Capstone Press, 2020.

Gilbert, Sara. *Spinosaurus*. Mankato, Minn.: Creative Education, 2019.

ON THE WEB

FACTSURFER

Factsurfer.com gives you a safe, fun way to find more information.

1. Go to www.factsurfer.com.

2. Enter "spinosaurus" into the search box and click 🔍.

3. Select your book cover to see a list of related content.

INDEX